Tasting the Dust

*For Anne & Henry –
with gratitude for our
family heritage –*

*Jean Janzen
Apr. 8, 2000*

Tasting the Dust

poems by Jean Janzen

Jean Janzen

Good Books
Intercourse, PA 17534
800/762-7171

Acknowledgments

Grateful acknowledgment is made to the editors of the following publications where these poems first appeared:

Burning Light, Christian Century, Christianity & Literature, Great River Review, Image, Kairos, Mars Hill Review, The Mennonite, Mennonite Life, Mennonite Quarterly Review, Poetry ("Claiming the Dust" and "Magnolia"), and *Rhubarb*.

Special thanks to the National Endowment for the Arts for the grant that made some of these poems possible.

Cover watercolor by Rollin Pickford
Design by Dawn J. Ranck

TASTING THE DUST
Copyright © 2000 by Jean Janzen
International Standard Book Number: 1-56148-301-X
Library of Congress Catalog Card Number: 00-024844

All rights reserved. Printed in the United States of America.
No part of this book may be reproduced in any manner,
except for brief quotations in critical articles or reviews, without permission.

Library of Congress Cataloging-in-Publication Data
Janzen, Jean.
   Tasting the dust : poems / by Jean Janzen.
     p. cm.
   ISBN 1-56148-301-X
   I. Title.

   PS3560.A5364 T37 2000
   811'.54–dc21   00-024844

for Gail, Scott, Jill, and Peter

Table of Contents

I. Window Facing South   3
    Claiming the Dust   4
    In Tule Fog   6
    August Nights   7
    Oranges in a Hard Time   8
    Monarchs in Winter   9
    Listening for the News   10
    Pomegranate   11
    The Mountain   12
    At Summer's End   15

II. Window Facing North   17
    Overflow   18
    Pinwheel   19
    Kindling   20
    Moth   21
    Motion   22
    Underwater   23
    Looking at Nilsson's *A Child Is Born*   24
    Markings   25
    Beginning Again   26
    Cellar Blues   27
    Just Go   29
    Getting It Right   30
    Variations   31
    Rooms   33

III. Window Facing East	35
The Language of Light	36
Triptych: After Ghent	40
After the Martyrs Exhibit	41
Reading the Fields	42
Isaiah Fifty-Three	43
Raising the Dust in Siena	44
The Lion's Eye	45
The Frescoes, Fra Angelico	47
IV. Window Facing West	53
Lakes	54
December 7, 1941	57
Child in Black	58
Sun Crest	59
October	60
Magnolia	61
Ice	63
Elegy in the Shenandoah Valley	65
Tasting the Dust	66
About the Poet	68

Part I

Window Facing South

"Young Girl with Water Pitcher" Vermeer

Caught in the motion
of opening the window,
she is held in uncertainty—
was that a voice rising

from the street, or someone
calling to her within the house?
One hand on the brass pitcher,
the other on the window latch,

she is suspended in the air
of spring which has filled
the room, ready to loosen
whatever is bound.

Claiming the Dust

Like nomads we come
to this subtropical valley,
our borrowed space
under the sun. Once
an ancient lakebed,
the July ground powders
under our feet, lifts
in puffs to welcome us.
The children rise, then
run out to pound acorns
under the oaks, calling
to each other from
their rings of stones.
Pale bird-of-paradise leans
out of its gravelly bed.
It takes dynamite to plant
an orange tree, our neighbor sighs.

This is our new home,
this valley's layered clay
which offers its sunbaked surface
to the scuffing of our feet,
as if our fragile lives
are enough to rouse the ages.
The slightest breeze, and the dust
becomes skittish, whirls
to settle in the next yard.
But mostly, stillness,

so that the beige siftings
are almost imperceptible.
Fig leaves in a talcum haze.

It is the night we finally learn
to claim. At dusk the children
float their sheets like flattened tents
and sprawl face-up into the warm
darkness, and we join them
in this rehearsal—a summer
night travel, the sky's black
curtains pinned back with stars.
That open stage.
This hard earth not our final holding
place after all, but the air
into which we sail,
breath by dusty breath,
toward a different shore.

In Tule Fog

It rises from the fields
like an ancient seabed
come back from the dead,
and hovers. Walking out
we join it, our hair and breath
becoming one with the past.
We're fish again, finning
through a millennium risen
for us, to cushion us,
to slow us for new sounds.

And she being born into this
diffusion, heaves from one float
into another—her mother's arms.
Her pulse flutters
in quick rhythm against
the slower, steady one.
And surrounding them both
is this rising of the ages,
as though she is not really new, but
fresh to us—given, so we can press
against our cheeks the wonder
of that time, or no-time,
from which she came, to which we go.

August Nights

These nights when first
fermentations sour the air,
I hear the semis churn
their loads in a great
continuous groan.
And I know that thousands
of pickers lie exhausted
under the meteor showers.
All day in the sun's
brutal press, the tails
of debris flared over them,
unseen, over the vineyards
where they knelt
in the suffocating rows,
knives flashing.
But when we lie down
at last, each of us
in our separate weariness,
we see the burning flowers,
some traveling the whole arc
of the sky. We forget
about the jagged mass
of stone and metal,
a mile wide, riding loosely
in an orbit over us.
But sometimes in our dreams
that cold weight sweeps close,
and we awaken with clenched
hands, praying for the sun
and its labors to blind us
through another day.

Oranges in a Hard Time

Midwinter in the fog
oranges sweeten and fall—
lamp-glow on the grass,
then mold and mush.
For weeks I let them fall,
felt their fall.
Hour after sodden hour,
no desire to move. Cars
in and out of the driveway,
slam of doors. Birds bickering.
Let the rot do its work.
But then, what was that turn
toward light?
I was on my knees gathering
the firm and golden ones,
pulling them one after another
from the tree's dark hollows
to fill my mouth and arms.

Monarchs in Winter

To see these later generations
of last year's butterflies clustered
in the same eucalyptus trees

is what you want for your own,
but not that blind instinct,
that cost of survival—the path

north littered with broken wings.
The unremitting struggle.
And yet, to choose the right current

above the flashing ocean,
to smell the salt spray's edge.
To know the wide light, where

it intersects with their own,
so that they turn inland in time
to that unfamiliar home.

Listening for the News

Here in the west our news
comes from the Sierra, as it did
for the settlers last century
who galloped for an hour,
then found no one home,
the mountains their steadiest neighbors.
An isolation and distance
that gathers this summer morning
into a huge stillness.
What we learn is to wait,
knowing that the snow collected
on the high ridges will finally
give up to the sun and come down,
thrumming through the city in deep
canals. The children, unaware,
spill outdoors calling to each other.
They build teepees under dusty oaks,
and dig among the roots.
But the mothers sit motionless
with coffee cups, listening.
And at evening when they call
their children home, their voices echo
with a vibrating timbre, the news
of a distant roar, of scoured rocks,
and the loneliness of trees,
a calling which cuts into the hazy dusk
of the street and hovers there.

Pomegranate

This long valley caught
between two ranges,
this ancient seabed.
Nothing stirs in the scorched
fields, and still
our gardens swell, drinking
deeply from hidden
wells and streams.
So that in autumn a ripeness
hangs sweet and heavy
among brittle leaves—
seedy fig like a scrotum
in my hand, olives and walnuts
dropping as flocks
of starlings feast
and bicker in the trees.
The pomegranates won't fall;
their hides split and open
like books, rows
of ruby seeds clinging
to parchment. I clip one
and begin the crush,
suck the dark astringencies,
spit the seeds.
And I do a little jig,
clapping the air
with my stained hands.

The Mountain

From their cool, shaded rooms
we carried our children into the sun's glare,
past the burned hills,
and into the immense canyon.

We lifted them, pointing.
The river roared, battering
and shining in its swiftness,
and the walls it had made through

millennia stood taller than the world.
This is home, we said,
but they couldn't hear us.
Not until we carried them

back into their safe beds
did our voices enter them again.
Sleep, we whispered,
and stepped back into

our own solitudes, spaces
that couldn't hold us now,
but vibrated outward without end.

• • •

In spring the first slopes
are lacy with snowdrops, lupine, and fiddleneck
in a wild band of curve and curl—
the whole field bending
to lure us up and into the mountain's
huge embrace, up to the silence
of a high meadow's chilled nightfall,
the sudden precipice, and its white peak
like the Sanctus, overhead.
Over its granite lap, the mountain
has made a bed for us all,
pine-fragrant with dew gathering
for our lips, a place we had only
imagined until we entered like a child.
For the mountain calls the child,
the one who awakens early, who hears
the small sounds of seekers beside the
        streams.
In the silence of dawn, the rustle of leaves
where the chickaree leaps, the cracking
of seeds, the jay's blue streak.
No one sees him turn his back to the
        campground;
he doesn't hesitate, but follows
the source, pumping his arms in a run
before he pauses to turn back,
and discovers he has lost his way.

• • •

Where is home?
Is it this magma cooled and lifted,
the rocky ledge where poppies cling,

the roaring river cutting in,
and the peak with its icy distance
and sustenance?

Or is it our ancient valley seabed
which the mountain feeds,
where cotton bolls thicken and vines

swell with grapes?
Grace and necessity, the endless paradox.
Hungry, we open our mouths and arms,

and there, over the other's shoulder
we see the mountain, its craggy peak crowned
and waiting, even when it is hidden among
        clouds.

At Summer's End

The sweet run ends with the shutdown
gates at Pine Flat Dam.
And Fancher Creek begins its slow drain
into silence. It is inevitable,
the mountain's gift of snow-water
measured out. And then
what has been lost and discarded
reveals itself in the empty bed—
bicycle, mattress, the carcass of a dog.
I want the creek to run all year,
the singing that carries secrets away
to the sea, and buries them.
But even the Pacific returns
the lost—a diver, once, on the beach
where my children played, his black
suit glistening like a seal.
This spring a seven-year-old girl
spilled out into the lake
and hasn't been found. She had been
dragging her hands in the icy blue,
laughing, and no one saw what the clouds
held until the wind was unleashed.
That lake feeds the creek where I walk,
the sinking creek, that green music
which can't keep its secrets
because it has to stop. Because
a gift must be received to be a gift.
The whole thing. The truth of it.

Part II

Window Facing North

"Maidservant Pouring Milk" Vermeer

*She will spend her lifetime
in rooms, confined
to bread, table, wool,*

*and a narrow stream of milk.
Long tables of guests wait
somewhere, her children bang spoons*

*against their empty bowls,
and what she was given is
a rough pitcher, a window,*

*bread, and an apron
which grows deeper
in the folds of indigo blue,*

*all of it held
in a pale morning light,
her whole body pouring.*

Overflow

Today the young swallows
are practicing their flights
streaking in and out

in frantic patterns
from their mud nests under
the bridge. Their cries echo

over the high water of the creek,
an urgent calling from their silken
bodies, like an overflow.

Once we saw a tourist version
of "Swan Lake" danced on a stage
so small, the principals repeated

their patterns in tight circles.
And at the end the need and joy
collapsed for lack of space.

Our stories are too big
for our bodies. Our first heartbeat
is spill-over, and we are born

in a rush of water and cries.
With our whole body we lift
our first vowels to the air—

a stream, pressing
from a place we do not know.

Pinwheel

Verse means "to turn," the line
striving towards its end
which then seeks its beginning.

Last things first, as though
time itself knows where it began.
My mother, ninety-five years old,

is dying. "It's like a dream,
my life," she says, closing
her eyes, "like it really didn't happen."

And my newborn grandson opens
his eyes in unbelief—
these shapes, this shifting light.

Somewhere deep within the seed
this other seed, its shadows turning,
a wheel which opens its wings

from that non-dream
we try to imagine, around which
my poems circle—

that pin which holds time
against the wind for a brief,
bright whirring on the end of a stick.

Kindling

First sounds are first light,
translation for the shifting face,
the wall from which he drinks.
Pitches and sibilants become names,
unlocking doors. And when
the father murmurs, my child,
rubbing the boy's scalp until
it sparks, he hands him
match and kindling. Amazing
that we hold such fire,
that we are trusted with it.
And that child rouses
in the pre-dawn dark, even
as his father sleeps, descends
the stairs and reaches into
the cold, black mouth of the stove.
He blows his name over the first,
small flames, not only for his own
deep shivering, but for the others
when they rise.

for Allan

Moth

All night she pressed her body into
those factories of honey
for her very life. The lilies
welcomed her like lights, and the kitchen
globe called to her. Now she falls,
loose and powdery, from the curtain's
fold, shed-velvet, brevity of wing.

Maia in her house works her scissors
through pale cloth for the curled
antenna. She will fold the edge
of wing exactly for her invisible
stitches. I buy it for a pillow—
one moth for my ear to rub against
in winter—for the memory of jasmine
and the suck of nectar so deep,
you forget where your children are.

Motion

Gold and white, the angels cruised
the far spaces until your brush
dipped into thick acrylic and stopped them.
And from the water, a school
of dolphins leaps and stays—
the way you want your constant
body jerks to stop for the held
gesture, the control.
You turn your face to the wall;
your limbs lash out.
You have stopped nothing,
not the surf's roar, not
the black sunflowers in their dance,
or even these angels.
They keep drifting off, you say.

My hand writing this is steadier
than yours, but in the end
all is motion gathering.
And what is held is vibrating
like the winter finches in their
scarlet quarrel, and the amaryllis
which leans toward them from the other
side of the glass, huge throats open.
These vowels I fasten down
want to fly, as if these shapes
we give to sense, these shades
of blue and gold, make their own paths,
and you and I can only gaze
at what flashes by.

for Chad

Underwater

Sometimes a note is so clear
and high, I feel I am underwater,
the boy singing Auden's words,
pleading for the children,
the white-crowned sparrows' trillings
thickening my throat, late
afternoon in the orange trees
as the shadows swallow them.
Men and women who walk
fully-clothed into the surf
and don't turn back.
At the coast seagulls calling
"Come, come," and little Rachel
who fought for breath, but finally
drank the beautiful pool,
persuaded again, as at birth,
to let this world hold her.

Looking at Nilsson's *A Child Is Born*

Shrimp-curl, dark dot
under the mouth, spine like thread,
the skull a shadowed room

where thought and speech wait,
hushed and electric with
the pulse of mother's breath.

The mysteries of neuron and synapse
are branching in the buds
of the hands, the carved ear,

and the eyes—
eye of the eye,
ear of the ear,

the child who will sit hunched
over a classroom desk
to write on an April morning:

"I am an eagle
high in the air.
I can hear the flowers roar."

Markings

They come home with school papers flapping
in their hands, wings for civilization.
They smell like wind,

grounded in their bodies. I kiss them,
admire the strokes, the rows
of o's, save the best from year to year,

like the layered leaf-fall. Like
the botany booklet of my school years,
the pages filled with the wet green

of summer's trees—maple, box elder,
ash, and that catalpa leaf which I loved,
its thick veins, the way it overfilled

the page. Oh, I know it will all be buried,
pressed into rock at last. And yet,
somehow those markings loosen out of time.

What the children printed, bold—
*Yesterday I caught a dragonfly,
and then I let it go*—is saved, somewhere,

the place we enter after death.
That book of leaves.
And on the front, our names.

Beginning Again

All day the mountain aspens
gossiped about this world,
and the stream sang off-key.

At nightfall stars spilled out
heavy as fruit. Not until
we lay in our tents did we hear

the commotion, the crack
of branches and crushed garbage
cans—hunger with its black claws

banging the drums of alarm.
We drew up our legs
and slowed our breathing,

we listened to the shadow's
desperation—the bear
who had slept her long, musty dream

until she once again smelled
this world. Then she rose,
clumsy and half-blinded, toward

our offerings, fueled by one thing—
the certainty that something
within her needed to be saved.

Cellar Blues

I sing the harmony of summer jars,
of rusted keys and tools forgotten
under the sloping doors.
These are the tunes of the secret ear,
the cellar blues lost between
rows of canned plums and oozing walls.
I play the whole keyboard of cellars
as I sing—whitewashed ones
and dirt dugouts, bleached sheets
rolling out of the washer's mouth
and caught above the muddy floor,
songs of warped soundboards
and yellowed dissonance.
Even the church had a basement—
cool fragrance of body-earth
where cake and the coffeepot's tune
blended with roses and the dampness
of brides, a hymn for our appetites
which hold a key to the staircase.
I pry the stubborn lids of jars
sealed against taste for decades
and moan—glad blues, pungent
and dark blues, hot tomato harmonies
and watermelon pickle songs
with a slow, jazzy bass rhythm
of potatoes popping their eyes.

The pipes thump along and drip
staccato on curled shoes, the jars
join in, clinking shoulder to shoulder
in a brand new key of B-sharp minor
until the ceiling shakes and sifts
its dust into the amazed cellar-ear,
that fertile, inscrutable ear
which now flings its doors open
and leads me into the blinding light.

Just Go

Go to the other side.
Take the narrow bridge, the one

without the handrail.
Balance over the water's chorus

of voices and cross over
where the great oaks lean,

listening. Walk there
beside the wavering flicker

and you may hear, at last,
a separate voice, the call

of a child, or singing from the barn—
your brother's song of the fox hunt

in a run of hoofbeats and laughter,
as though light can be caught.

Keep following that light, even as
the water drains into cotton fields,

even though tonight the hounds
will whine in their dreams.

for Henry

Getting It Right

Three black turkey vultures
in the top of our cedar today
stare down at me, close.
Those circling the hills
are hand-span, but these
are the bent elders, judging.
"O Divine Redeemer" my sister sang
over and over, trying to get
everything right—tone, attack,
breath control, and I pressed
the piano keys, Gounod's melody
straining. What have we in us
to want perfection, to think
we can get it right?
And what is right on a day like this,
when choice is wide as the sky,
the scent of deodors stinging
the nostrils?
                      These vultures see
that my heart is still beating.
They'll soon stretch their awful necks
and flap away, easily reaching
those clear highways where they
will circle like winged hearses
and wait, then float back down
to wade in the spilled bodies,
tearing and feasting.
My sister and I will make careful
choices, but at the end nothing
will be perfect. Pardon, we'll cry,
trying to get it right.

Variations

Bach in summer, quail running
   through the yard. His thirty
      variations, his twenty children.

I listen as I work at the kitchen
   window, watch the chicks follow
      their parents, racing from cover

to cover. Bach's wife sighs—
   the baby awakens crying,
      older ones scuffle in the doorway,

and he continues inking notes
   over the undergirding bassline,
      notes that meander, skittish, until

he hears the pattern around
   one simple melody. One variation,
      then thirty, a moonful—

our daily labor and the body's
   demands. Menses sticky again
      after breastfeeding, the brief

intervals of silence, and that
   one octave of tones, erudite,
      detached, calling us to replay it

a thousand ways, to enlarge it
   with translations from the inner ear.
      We choose to listen, or not.

Bach perspires over the keys,
    not getting it right, tries again.
        Outside, the summer dust rises

and settles on the ivy—
    a scramble in the cedar shrub
        where the parents whistle

for flight. Forage and constant
    wariness moving up now into
        the safety of orange trees,

and Bach sitting still,
    listening to the beating
        of his heart.

Rooms

Rooms everywhere holding
our bodies, our memories,
walls and ceilings floating

around us in a balance
of matter and air.
Our mothers walking in

as we sleep. Emily
walking up the stairs
from the kitchen,

her hands white with flour.
The bundles of poems,
each one a mansion

of rooms. The meadow's
blue ceiling, sunflower's
treasury packed tight.

The pain inside the oak.
The rain unlocking
the mountain.

Part III

Window Facing East

"Woman in Blue Reading a Letter" Vermeer

> *The landscape comes to her*
> *in a room where she waited, where now*
> *she stands beside two empty chairs,*
>
> *table, and map, gripping the folded*
> *page with both hands. The message*
> *is a mountain range with valleys,*
>
> *fields, and inscrutable lakes*
> *vibrating against the page.*
> *All this in one voice.*
>
> *Now he is present in her face,*
> *in the color blue,*
> *the silk of her jacket,*
>
> *and the chairs of stretched*
> *leather, holding the shadows.*

The Language of Light

Weary of war, artists in Holland
lifted the slow fire
of pewter onto canvas, the wild silk

of tulips, and those new maps,
which on Vermeer's walls
held peaceful borders behind

the breathing bodices of women.
Heroism in the texture
of brick, fine wool, copper gleam,

and a housewife's face, open
as a waterlily. Vermeer's bones
and those broken soldiers'

float in the same soggy earth,
the stone markers only approximate.
Now my own feet float

on this watery country where light
cannot be divided from light,
no matter how thick the earthen dams,

this country where earth itself
holds light—the pouring milk,
the porcelain cheek of the maid,

and the city of Delft, its towers
and brick held between sky and water
by the artist's eye, by cerulean blue

and dots of white stroked upon
crushed and woven flax, the threads
still holding the vowels of the sun.

• • •

Sometimes it speaks in music,
like this carillon spilling
its barrels of tones around us.

High noon, and these rich vibrations
suddenly drop from a tower
where the player presses bells

into motion, all their dark hollows
bright now and falling.
The notes tumble recklessly

into the spaces around this old
weigh-house for cheese (once
the Church of the Holy Ghost).

They pour over the brass scales,
bright hats, and piled circles
of Edam and Gouda, as if measurement

and order are not complete
without this wild joy
which now enters me, finding

a hidden place where light
has waited all my life,
ripe and ready to ring.

• • •

And in the green of Friesland
where Boniface arrived in 775,
slopping through the mud

with the Book in his hands.
I stand on the mound where
my frightened ancestors murdered him,

where they wailed their songs
in December, trying to keep the sun
from sinking, the sea moaning

in accompaniment. They didn't kill
that light. The pages turn
in the paintings of Memling and Van Eyck,

all those faces reading.
The pages burn in Haarlem,
1557, ashes lift off

the scorched skull of the bookseller;
men toss words into the fire
and others run off, arms full.

The hunger to know, and the stooped figure writing. The inked letters unraveling out of the first

illuminated "I," the beginning of this world.

Triptych: After Ghent

1564, and they are pulling Mayke
from the castle's dungeon, up
the winding stone steps, dragging
her chains. The wheels groan
toward the stake where she will
be burned, toward the watching crowd
where her small son stands.
She reaches out and places
a pear in his hand.

• • •

Just across the river in Van Eyck's
triptych, Eve is looking at Adam.
Her arm will reach across the middle panel,
will brush against the lamb
who shivers on the throne.
The centuries are kneeling, watching.
The apple is fresh and glazed with oil.

• • •

Now I stand in the archives
holding Mayke's pear,
a brown oval, light as ash.
I hold the strength
of her last glance—
her son's pale face,
the stopped river.
And I hold the tree,
its blossoms flaring
around her feet.

After the Martyrs Exhibit

The way the sparrows sing
in the bushes, you would think
that no one could torture another,
especially this hour before dinner
as evening spreads its silk cloth.
We had seen the copper plates
under display lights, each line
etched to evoke remembrance—
acid for my conscience.
Rolled ink, the press on paper,
and there she stands,
her skirt flaming, mouth singing.

We dip hummus and swallow,
talk easily as evening folds.
Sliced bamboo driven under fingernails.
The jeering. The betrayal of dawn.
I never said I could do it.

Reading the Fields

> *". . . through mouth and pen,
> with possessions and life,
> with life and death."* Menno Simons

The tulips unfold their pages
    field after field in brilliant
        illuminations. Even under

pewter skies, they glow
    for weeks, red, yellow and purple
        bolts of silk unrolled like a story

of happily-ever-after. But then
    the harvest, bright words
        cut down and raked into piles.

Brief singing.
    Only the bulbs remain, hidden
        and nourished by dying leaves,

each one a lit window among
    the dark trees—someone
        leaning into the next word.

Isaiah Fifty-Three

Van Gogh stopped painting
the black Bible.

Instead he took
black apart, color

by color, and let
its strands pulse

and moan in chairs
and stars, in trees

and ears of wheat.
Grief acquainted

with blue. Rejection
in sulphurous green.

He did it for us
so we could look

if we dared, taste
the ache, let it sizzle

under our own skin.
So we could be healed.

Raising the Dust in Siena

The way the horses race
in the piazza, you would think
they are pursued, pounding
and circling wildly, manes
flying with the dust.
This city where St. Catherine,
"that unmanageable child,"
tamed herself into silence,
remaining in one room for years
until she heard the words,
go now.
                Tonight these circling
streets echo with horses
and children, and the footsteps
of spectators. Soon darkness
will fold its history over us,
but will we sleep, here where
Catherine's bones lie enshrined,
her work undone, one foot given
away to Venice? Cups still empty,
treaties broken. This century
moving toward its end in an awkward
spin, the rumble rising, and the crowd
waving its bright flags of division.

The Lion's Eye

In Venice we turn our heads this way,
then that, and it glints back.
Sun on water, we say, but it is
the eye of the winged and ancient lion.

It winks from palace arches, towers,
the soft and glittering mosaics
in their shadowed domes, from the violin
singing Verdi, and my hand on the glass.

The bones of St. Mark lie hidden
among stolen gold and the broken
hulls of ships. The pilings shift
beneath us, reeds shiver.

Masks everywhere, and the eye
gleams through. For the story
is still being written—
in the shopkeeper's gesture,

in the flesh of Titian's paintings,
his reds and blues. And in the church
where Bellini's Holy Infant sits
on his mother's lap,

it shines in her eyes.
Refuge and loss, this child
like water on whom we float
until he takes us in.

Open your lap, the story goes,
open the gates. We write it
as we look and as we leave,
and the lion's eye never closes.

The Frescoes, Fra Angelico

The Annunciation

First, the gazing, without words,
his eyes two clear wells
and she a window. Her folded arms
will fall in silence
for she is becoming air itself
with his look, dispersing, floating
like light above the carved arches
of the portico.

• • •

But then he speaks.
The words tumble out

like stones—an avalanche
to topple walls,

to make a bridge, to lift
an arch, a leaf, a scroll,

to make the space
which holds her here.

• • •

This is the moment of
stone and air, the Word
wheeling into her
the way words do—
flight and density.
Hot stone, molten cell,
its syllables of I Am—You Are,
whirling. The gravity of love.

The Nativity

The infant has just slipped out,
naked and haloed, onto ethereal straw.

But no, not straw. It is a bed
of golden needles for his baby skin.

His mother, heavily draped and in awe,
does not notice, nor Joseph,

but the donkey and ox raise their heads
from the feeding trough, expecting his cry.

Mary, in a moment, will rescue him,
will wrap him, murmuring, breasts dripping.

Angelico knew that this is the moment before,
when nakedness is light, too hot to hold.

Presentation in the Temple

Simeon leans away from Mary,
her open reaching hands.
He gazes into the child's eyes,

holding him tight, a swaddled
cocoon, his golden head exposed,
his little red boots.

The child gazes back as if
he understands the words *light*
and *sword*—a far look.

Mary will reclaim the child
with her porcelain hands
from which, one day, he will slip

unnoticed, and she will search
for the rest of her life.
She will call and call

among the bright shards,
turning her head
this way, then that.

The Sermon on the Mount

Jesus is choosing
his words. The time
is short, the sky gray.
The twelve listen, absorbing,
even Judas with black halo.

The plaster is beginning
to dry. What are
the essential words?
His face is in shadow,
his words are becoming
the mountain.
It is glowing.
The disciples
do not know
they are sitting
on fire.
His face
grows darker,
the last pigments
sinking in.

Noli Me Tangere

Mary Magdalene is kneeling by the open
tomb, reaching out. She wants to touch him.

Over Christ's shoulder, a rough garden hoe,
the other hand reaching,

golden hair on his shoulders, his pierced
feet doing a light step in the grass.

He would slip out through the gate, unnoticed,
but now this woman with her sweet aroma,

that unbearable skin on skin.
His heart is beating

in the cracked plaster. Angelico's brush
is making little flower-strokes.

Their hands are only inches apart.
He wants to touch her.

Part IV

Window Facing West

"Lady Weighing Gold" Vermeer

*Late afternoon
in a shadowed room,
the only light, her body*

*and the glint of pearls.
She has turned her back
to the painting on the wall—*

*The Last Judgment, black and blurred.
Nor is the judgment in her hands,
the scales balancing.*

*It rests in her calm face,
her delicate wrists,
her skin holding the light.*

Lakes

Every Sunday, as we drove past,
it was a different thing—
a plate of porcelain, thick,
under which fish moved,
searching; a keyhole
shimmering, waiting
for the swinging door;
or a mirror glaring so that
I was blinded
unless I turned away
just enough to catch
a glimpse of the real.
Always it was a glimpse
until I entered it,
until one day
I felt the stones
under my feet,
the slimy grass waving,
and the water lifting me.

• • •

Sometimes we would picnic
above the lake on the high
slope, girls together.

We wove crowns of dandelions,
our limbs and laughter light,
and yet we felt a pull under the grass.

Somehow we knew, at ten
and eleven, the weight
of water and its demands,

so that the lake below us
became ours—the way
it kept its arms open,

and filled, the way
it would feed the hidden
spaces waiting beneath it.

• • •

When my father baptized
the teenage girls, they wore white
and walked in one by one.
His starched shirt sleeves softened
as he lifted the lake into their hair.
And they walked out one by one,
sloshing against the heaviness,
their dresses clinging to their hips,
their bare feet gathering
the muddy sand, as the trinity
shone in their hair, which they
kept bound until bedtime,
when it fell around their bare
shoulders, and filled the shadows
of their rooms.

• • •

Never had we floated
on such clarity as on the Königsee,
a liquid diamond holding us
high in the Alps.
Only a faint ripple, as when we
barely breathe, our bodies
an interruption of depth
and stillness, our eyes burning,
our hands dipping into that light,
so cold and pure, we knew
that only a mountain could hold it.

• • •

Each spring we find Lost Lake
again, thickening with horsetail
and dragonflies. And every year
our children bring their nets.
Where nothing moved in the heat
of last August they now join
the blur of spring; all afternoon
they splash and call.
So that at dusk, when they enter
the car, the lost is held in their skin,
in the swinging of their limbs, and in
the wings battering against the sides of the jar.

for Anne

December 7, 1941

The child hears the words "Pearl Harbor"
and imagines a white iridescence.
Outside it is snowing, winds
whipping against window glass.

All is white to the child
except her own warmth under the lamp
where she moves paper dolls
in a slow waltz. Her brothers,

in the chill of the doorway, talk
of bombs and fire. But she
sees pearls held in a huge bowl
where ships glide in and anchor,

a plenitude from which she pulls
a string to wrap around the slim
necks of the dancers. The voices
continue—the roar of planes,

the floating dead. She lifts her hand
up to the lamp, its red rivers
and its pulse, then layers the smiling
dolls into the box, and closes the lid.

Child in Black

Near Moscow your parents whisper
about a body bag. One stream
of milk from a tin pulls you up
from starvation's well,
And then, the ship's journey
without parents—little girls
alone, deep in the hold,
the vomiting into blackness.
How deep can you go, spiraling down?

And when you arrive in the new country
at last, no one is at the train station
except the moonless night.
Your footsteps echo on the planks
until someone, something
leads you to a home, where
in the morning you rinse
your ragged underwear
in a basin of tears and light.

for Anne Friesen

Sun Crest

Home is wherever you lay
your carpet down, the rug dealer
told us in Baku. That free life,
shifting with wind and sand.
And yet, the ancient patterns,
tight knots to create
each vine and rose.
The young girls' fingers
follow the design exactly—
under Allah and the swirl
of stars, the binding.

Child of immigrants, I claim
this valley as mine. I walk
the dusty rows of peach orchards
sucking my friend's sweet Sun Crests.
The trees, brittle and braced,
still drink heavily from irrigation
flow. This earth, worn carpet,
home for awhile.

Possession—its knots, its sorrows,
the trees pulled out and burning
at last in a field fire.
We taste and we gaze, but what
we finally hold in our empty hands
is what we glimpsed—a memory
of beauty and sweetness like a secret home,
where, when we enter, someone
calls us by a new name.

October

Now the blind for hunters
is visible in the bare maple.
Last week your uncles hunched there,
listening among the rattle
of leaves. And the heart
of the deer was humming.

Today our feet swish through
the bright, fallen taffeta,
a cacophony before the slope
toward barren stillness.
We can't save all the music.
The cabin is filled with antlers,

and how much can earth hold?
It's a matter of cadence
among extravagance.
Not hiding, but walking,
bold, into the death of summer
and into the clearing, singing.

for Julia

Magnolia

These days my mother rarely notices
the magnolia outside her door,
its cupped, white blooms,
hardly glances at her potted plants.
Her small chest heaves,
her sparrow-bones gather on the couch.
This valley is too dry; her skin
has become parchment. She hears
the hiss of failure—prairie dust,
the thin wail of children.
Clinging to a drop from the bent straw,
she refuses satiating gulps,
too lavish now, like branches leaning
with their many hands.

I open the door to let the June night
come in, the magnolia crowded with fragrance.
Then the mockingbird begins, sings
his tireless aria. Rudolfo's lament?
Which way should Mimi turn her head?
All night he continues, borrowing
my mother's breaths phrase by phrase.
He wants to hold her here, as if
to see her rise, wobbly and rumpled,
but faithful to the singer,
the lover we want to believe
will never forsake us.
For this is his season.

But birds when they die
find hidden places, sigh invisibly

into leaves. For it is the air
itself which finally claims us,
drawing our last exhalations
into its reckless burning, this air
which we have borrowed since
our first stunned gasp.

My mother stirs and breathes
unevenly into this night's betrayal,
its leaf-rasp and empty pods.
Her hand is pale against mine,
and her bruises flare in the dark.

Ice

1

My mother dies in upheaval,
emaciated. Hollow eyes,

mouth like stone.
She is an empty house.

No kindling
for the iron-cold stove.

No one rattling
the pots in the morning.

2

Her voice is a needle, calling.
A stitch this time tears nine,
and the cold wind howls.
Her feet on the treadle faster now;
pins in her mouth.
I am too slow. She can't see me coming.

3

Her hot flat-iron sizzled
a Gothic arch through
the thick porch window ice

so I could watch
the rink at recess—
the kids circling, falling.

My breath kept the glass
in a blurred thaw, and I saw
what I would become—one of them.

Now she looks through,
she without breath, her lips frozen,
her hands still at last.

I can't see in.
I want her hot again, working
through the icy layers

so my eyes can see hers,
clear blue with recognition.

Elegy in the Shenandoah Valley
for my mother, Anna Wiebe, 1898-1994

Here you are earth itself.
I test my shoulder against
the misty layers and float,

strangely at home. Last leaf-fall,
pieces of your bright dresses
in untended piles, and you stripped down.

I fall asleep in your violet light
and awaken to a storm rolling in
from the west, coming to do the work

that shapes this place.
A pounding against my windows,
wild music that scours the bones.

And then the moon, speechless
to see me here, to see us both
ancient now. The river rides

through me, dragging its silt
in a slow murmur. Not the rush
and glance of your hands,

but what lay hidden and waiting
in you. All those years a gathering
of streams for such a place

as this, where you hold me
and let me go.
Where I will find you again.

Tasting the Dust

The way he brings it in,
leaves falling from his hair,
then kisses me, you would think

that gardening is pleasure,
which he says it is, digging deep
to kill bermuda roots, piercing

his hands on roses.
Sweat drips into my eyes
from his forehead, physician

curing himself with soil.
Sometimes I join him, raking
the pages of leaves, but the garden

is his, the place which gathers
struggles from his hands
and returns its own—

the story of dust, an origin
so deep and dense, it rose
like fire to make the mountain,

a narrative of tumble
and breakage from its sides,
the wet roar of ages

under the slow beat of the sun.
The mountain offering itself
in mud, sticks and stones

for his spade, his touch,
to make of it a shape and fragrance,
to taste the center of this earth.

About the Poet

Jean Wiebe Janzen was born in Saskatchewan, was raised in the midwestern United States, and now lives in Fresno, California.

She completed her undergraduate studies at Fresno Pacific University and received the Master of Arts at California State University of Fresno. Her previous books are *Words for the Silence* (1984), *Three Mennonite Poets* (1986), *The Upside-Down Tree* (1992), and *Snake in the Parsonage* (1995).

Janzen teaches poetry writing at Fresno Pacific University and at Eastern Mennonite University in Virginia.